MEDITATION SUPERHERO
EMPOWERING GUIDED MEDITATIONS FOR CHILDREN

Louis **LEGRAND**

With illustrations by **Bettina BRASKÓ**

To Cyrille.

CONTENT

INTRODUCTION

The history of this book is quite extraordinary. At first, this book had been dedicated to all the superheroes of this planet as a tool to develop a mind capable of managing their superpowers. However, it indirectly led to many self-discoveries about superpowers in the general population. Not long after the first version had been published, people found themselves developing extra-sensorial powers. They found new energy centers in their bodies, as well as an ability to manage fears and doubts. They soon began to feel connected and protected. In light of this development, a version of the book that is easier to read was released.

The technique remains the same. Superheroes still train their minds in this way, and it does not require much effort, because superheroes have many other things to do after all! You'll just have to imagine amusing things and pay attention to your body; that's it. Superheroes don't do anything else when they train their minds.

The instructions are to be followed preferably in a quiet room, with your eyes closed or semi-closed. Everything is made for you to have fun along the way. Doing superhero jobs should always be fun!

The time of the exercises can change according to the reader's preference, but remember that everything is made to be easy to follow.

During the sessions, you may find it difficult to stay focused. It is not unusual to have a ton of other thoughts rushing through your head at the same time when you try to follow the instructions. Do not worry; let such thoughts pass, just like you would watch cars passing by on the street. The most important thing is to come back to the instructions calmly and be highly motivated to train in the same way as superheroes regularly do.

One last thing - it is very important for you to have no hesitation in sharing how you felt with your eyes closed or semi-closed after each exercise with the reader. You can even write to me so that your comments will help other super-children like you!

I wish you a very peaceful and amusing journey.

This book only provides guided meditation scripts. If you are new to meditation and mindfulness for children, please consider getting some additional knowledge with amazing books that present the benefits of meditation for children.

For my English-speaker readership, I cannot recommend enough Susan Kaiser Greenland's book: *The Mindful Child, How to Help your Kid Manage Stress and Become Happier, Kinder and More Compassionate.*

CHAPTER 1
THE REAL SOURCE OF ALL SUPERPOWERS

Welcome to this first meditation. Your training has now begun. We are going to use the same meditation technique that is assigned to superheroes when they start their mind-training program. The principle of this first session is to make superheroes aware of the real source of their powers. Whatever their unique superpowers might be, what superheroes all have in common is that they have to draw their gifted strengths from a particular location in their body. Within minutes, you are going to discover it by yourself. Remember that people from everywhere found out that they can access this source too, and there's no reason you can't. So let's start, shall we?

1. Find a place where you can either be seated or lie down in a very comfortable position. Choose the position that makes you feel the most relaxed. Take your time and don't rush things. It's very important for you to find a position you feel OK in.

2. Now start to breathe normally.

3. Then, put your hands on your knees if you are sitting or against your body if you are lying down. Remain as relaxed as you can.

4. Close your eyes now and continue to breathe normally. We are

ready to search for the source of all superpowers, a source every superhero knows about.

5. For you to do that, continue to breathe normally and first try to find out what part of your body is moving as you breathe. As for every living being, breathing has an impact on your body. Do you feel the wind in your nostrils as you breathe? Or do you feel your chest rising? Maybe it is your stomach! Maybe it's all three parts. Take a few breaths and take your time to find out which area of your body moves the most. Gently place your right hand on this zone. Try to feel the movement better.

6. Now place both hands on your belly for a few seconds.

7. Try to breathe harder, swallowing lots of air through the nose and spitting lots of air through the mouth.

8. The secret of superheroes is to breathe with the help of their belly. The source of all their superpowers is there, in their belly. Did you notice that your breath was actually taking place in that zone? If so, you are on a very good track to unleash your superpowers. However, you will have to continue to maintain this magical source and make it shine! Becoming a superhero takes a lot of work! If you didn't find your belly rising and falling, do not feel ashamed - it's our mission to discover and enhance the powers you've got inside you.

9. To make sure you do proper belly-breaths, imagine your belly swelling like a giant air balloon by taking a deep breath in through the mouth. Store as much air as possible in your belly that way. Once the giant air balloon in your belly is full, make the air go away by breathing out through the mouth.

10. Feel your hands on your belly as it deflates. Repeat this technique several times calmly, without forcing the breath. It is said that many superheroes take it the wrong way when they are beginning. They often try to inflate their belly at the same time as they draw air out the mouth, which as you can figure is very complicated. How could an air balloon be floating in the air without

air inside of it?

11. Once you have mastered this technique, imagine expelling air through your entire body this time. Imagine your arms and legs stretching with the help of your breath. Imagine your muscles growing while you breathe. By doing so, you are tricking your mind so it will give you as much power as if you were a giant person.

12. Congratulations, you've just learned to foster the deep source of all superpowers. You can now breathe more slowly again, putting air in your belly while you breathe in, and putting air out of your belly while you breathe out.

13. Now, with your eyes still closed, begin to pay attention to the things around you; do you notice any noises? How does the contact of your body with the chair, sofa or bed feel like? Breathe normally and enjoy the calm feeling that the discovery of the source of all superpowers gave you.

14. Open your eyes and take some time to enjoy the feeling of calm and restfulness.

15. Every time you want to activate a superpower in this book, you'll have to give your body some time to connect with this technique. Superheroes simply refer to it as the "superhero's breath."

- NAMASTE -

(NAMASTE is the superhero formula often used
after training. It's a thankful message directed to your
mind since it makes you stronger.)

CHAPTER 2
ACTIVATING YOUR X-RAY VISION

Once you feel comfortable enough with the source of all superpowers, which is the "superhero's breath", it is now time to actually find these other superpowers. We'll start with the X-ray vision. As soon as you find it, you'll immediately be able to see through things. Well, not ALL things. But you'll be able to see through your own body and that's pretty amazing. The better you know what is going on in your body, the better you can do what you want with it. Do you want to be able to feel calm when you need to? Do you want to be energized when you ask for it? Do you want to perform better in sports or with any of your hobbies? Well, everything must start with a deep look at your body! Superheroes know that pretty well. They always scan their body to look for any potential weakness that would likely put them in danger.

1. As we learned before in the "superhero's breath" session, you should find a place where you can be seated or lie down, feeling relaxed and comfy. Start to breathe at a normal pace, taking care of your belly swelling as you breathe in and deflating as you breathe out.

2. Keep breathing this way until you feel the "superhero's breath" going through your whole body.

3. Now we are going to call the "superhero's light" to come and guide you through your body. This light is so powerful that it can help you see through things as if you had actual X-ray vision. Repeat after me loudly: *"light of the hero, please come and guide me through my body."* Whenever you wish to activate the X-ray vision, you simply have to call this light. Such a powerful light is always with you; just ask it to help you.

4. Now feel the supernatural light illuminating your head. Feel its heat. The « superhero's light » will now illuminate all the parts of your body, provided that you focus on it.

5. Try to focus on your neck, feel how that light illuminates it; this light is as warm as the sunlight in summer.

6. Then feel the light on your chest… on your belly… then go back to your upper body, but focus on your back now; feel the light of the hero on your lower back, then on the upper arms… on the lower arm… on your hands. Feel the light illuminating your fingers, one by one.

7. Get the supernatural light to help warm up your legs… your calves… your feet… feel the light illuminating your toes, one by one.

8. Once the light has traveled through your whole body, imagine that your X-ray vision is now so strong that you can see through your entire body, every part being illuminated at the same time. Every part of your body that the light has touched is now ready to reveal what's inside of it. Feel your muscles under your skin that allow you to move forward and play. Feel your veins that carry life. Feel the course of your breath that makes your mind stronger. Feel this new X-ray vision power that will serve you in times of turmoil.

This light will help you know what is wrong, discover hidden wounds and thus will allow you to be more powerful. Say, *"Thank you light for making me see through things."*

9. It's now time to refocus your attention on the belly, so practice a last few « superhero's breaths ». Feel how your breath feels powerful, aided by the "superhero's light" that just skimmed over your whole body.

10. When you feel ready, open your eyes. You have just found your X-ray vision. Congratulations!

- NAMASTE -

CHAPTER 3
SWITCHING ON YOUR
SPONTANEOUS SLEEP BUTTON

Although all the activities in this book had at first been made to strengthen the mind of superheroes, a particular technique needs special attention. What I'm talking about is the power of "spontaneous sleep". This technique is especially useful for superheroes, as sleep allows them to purify their minds. With sleep, superheroes can completely empty their minds of all the negative energy they accumulated while being in contact with enemies and troublemakers.

For many reasons, sometimes superheroes are unable to sleep peacefully in their room or in a real bed. Think about a superhero for a second who is forced to go on a mission far away from home, or whose home was destroyed by a villain. These things can happen when you are a superhero! Learning to be able to fall asleep in any situation - regardless of how agitated and negative one's mind is - is therefore very important. It's now time for us to learn to use such a superpower in order to have as strong of a mind as superheroes do.

1. Find a place where you can lie down feeling relaxed and comfy. Start to breathe at a normal pace, taking care of your belly swelling as you breathe in and deflating as you breathe out.

2. Start by gently closing your eyes, and take deep breaths in that way. Remember that the "superhero's breath" helps you in aligning your body and mind so as to make them as powerful as those of superheroes'.

3. Now that you feel OK and relaxed, we are going to put every part of your body asleep to let them regenerate during the night. There is a very simple way to put the parts of your body asleep, and it is as easy as turning off a light in a room. It consists of simply tightening your muscles for a few seconds and releasing them for a few more. Your body is full of switches of this kind! Superheroes know them all, and they know that it is very useful for getting into a purifying resting state. Let's not wait any longer!

5. Tighten your feet a few seconds, then release them. Do you feel the tension accumulated throughout the day now escaping from your body? At the end only the purity of your mind sitting in your lightened body should remain. We want your body to be so light that it can lie on a beautiful cloud.

6. Tighten now and release your ankles, your calves… do the same to your lower legs, your knees and your belly. Tighten and release your chest, the top of your arms… now down your arms, then take care of your hands and your fingers. Tighten and relax your neck and finally your head. Every superhero has to go through these steps to feel on top of the world the next day. It's part of the job!

7. Now center your attention on your belly and apply the « superhero's breath ». Did you know that every night the air balloon of your body takes you on a protective cloud? Now imagine the air balloon you play with by breathing in and out flying up in the sky. Each deep breath you take makes it go higher. Your air balloon is lifting your body towards roofs and buildings. Finally, it lays you

down on a soft, warm and comfortable cloud that lulls you in the moonlight. You're now safe, protected by the stars; you can sleep and purify your mind like superheroes do every night.

8. Sweet dreams.

- NAMASTE -

CHAPTER 4
TRIGGERING YOUR SUPER BRAIN

Apart from learning, there is something else that is essential for you. To discover the world and fulfill their dreams, superheroes must also keep on learning how to act powerfully in the world and how to develop clever strategies. Much discipline is required for them, and as you can imagine, their timetables are indeed quite messed up by all kinds of events. There is nobody who really knows when superheroes must come and save us all! But to maintain the discipline needed to nurture and expand their brain, superheroes have got some nice tools. They can for example develop and connect to their "super-brain". The good news is that you've got one of those too! And you'll find it very helpful to help you focus and achieve your goals. A super-brain means working faster. It means having more free time for activities that matter the most. Are you interested in triggering your super-brain? Let's not waste any more time.

1. As we learned before in the "superhero's breath" session, find a place where you can be seated or lie down feeling relaxed and comfy. Start to breathe at a normal pace, taking care of your belly swelling as you breathe in and deflating as you breathe out.

2. After two complete and mindful "superhero's breaths", close your eyes and imagine before you a beach in summer. Don't worry, you're safe there, your family is close to you. Other children around you are smiling as they run in all directions. Listen to the waves and the laughter of the other kids.

In this setting you know that, like every superhero who seeks to trigger his super brain, you need to build a solid sand castle which is free of hazards. Your super brain grows stronger that way. So, take time to first imagine the castle you plan to build. Have in mind every detail of it. How many towers do you need? How big will it be? What kind of king and queen will inhabit it? And with whom?

3. Again, eyes closed, have a deep breath rooted in your belly. You can now choose to isolate yourself from the surrounding agitation. Maybe children on the beach are calling you to go play with them. It may also be that the water seems so pure and so warm that you feel like swimming a little. But you know you can do all these things later on. All that matters now is to be in the present moment and to focus on the sandcastle you are going to build away from all the commotion, sheltered from the wind.

Good news! A little further away you can see a remote place with a few people resting under the sun. Yet you know you're safe there; your family is not so far, you can reach them at any moment. This place is perfect - there is even a shovel and a bucket! The sand seems quite suited to build the castle you have in mind. It's time to build it now.

4. So do it. Block by block, as superheroes would to enhance their super-brain, you build the fantastic castle and you come back constantly to cement its foundations. Carry on, and keep in mind the very precise image of the castle you have been planning to build at the beginning.

5. The wind now gets stronger, but you stay strong and focused on your goal. You are rested, strong and patient, and your gestures are precise and responsive. When the wind is too strong, it is your

mission to use the "superhero breath" to face headwinds more efficiently. Visualize the agitation that grows with the wind, as such agitation threatens your castle, but you are breathing hard to ground yourself and finish your castle.

6. After some courageous efforts, a smile shows up on your face as you put the last block of the castle in place. Your patient and careful work have just resulted in a wonderful castle. Congratulations! It sure is work worthy of superheroes.

7. Now focus one last time on your breath, and thank your arms for having helped you build the castle. Thank your legs and your belly for having helped you withstand the wind. Finally, thank your brain for having directed your whole body so precisely.

8. Open your eyes. Nothing can stop you now. You have the discipline of a superhero. Every meditation about building the sandcastle teaches your brain to withstand bustle. With it, you can achieve any kind of goal with tremendous speed.

- NAMASTE -

CHAPTER 5

APPRECIATING YOUR INVINCIBILITY

In this chapter, we are going to learn a very useful technique that superheroes use when times get tough. Sure, superheroes are greeted by the crowd with tons of applause and cheers when they save the world from great perils. However, before all that, superheroes have to fight against many odds. Superheroes may encounter many setbacks and become doubtful. I'm sure you know of a superhero who had suffered many failures before their final triumph. Such failures make a superhero doubtful.

Am I really a superhero? Do I really deserve all the attention people give me? Who do I think I am to try to save the world? All these questions are bad for superheroes, because they do nothing but pollute their strong minds. They can make a superhero lose all courage even though they need it to overcome their own failures.

We also occasionally encounter times when things are not going in the direction that we would like them to. We, just like superheroes, often become doubtful. To regain our strength and find ourselves able to overcome this, we can make use of a powerful mind technique. Let's find out what it is. Let's discover our own super-ability to become stronger than failures.

1. As we learned before in the "superhero's breath" session, find a place where you can be seated or lie down feeling relaxed and comfy. Start to breathe at a normal pace, taking care of your belly swelling as you breathe in and deflating as you breathe out.

2. Once you are grounded with your mind ready to develop your superpowers, you can do as superheroes do: start complimenting yourself. This may seem uneasy and quite bizarre, but don't be shy, no one can judge you here. With your eyes closed, repeat these three sentences like a superhero: *"I am capable of great things. I have immense strength in me. I am neither better nor worse than the others, and just like everyone else, I can make beautiful things if I believe in myself."* Repeat it once again: *"I am capable of great things. I have immense strengths in me. I am neither better nor worse than the others, and just like everyone else, I can make beautiful things if I believe in myself."*

3. Now, with your eyes closed, recall one of your own or a friend's success. Remember that your friends are neither better nor worse than you. They all are human beings capable of great things like you. Imagine this success in great detail - the smiles on every face, the feeling of accomplishment led by the joy of having done something important. In periods of doubt, superheroes always call their past successes to gain courage. They also think about the successes of others, because they know that it sheds light on the potential of each of us to achieve great things.

4. The next step is to convert your past failures into victories. Nothing is easier than that. You are already equipped for that. You have the power of transforming painful past events into magic stairs inside yourself. Let's see how and why we need magical stairs.

5. Let's start by visualizing a past failure the same way you visualize a photograph. Observe this failure with no worries; you are safe here. Now touch the image mentally with your hands and have the following formula in mind: *"I have not been able to... it taught me that…"* Then uses the formula and complete it with the description of your past failure and the lesson it has taught you.

A superhero may say, *"I had not been able to save this person, it taught me that I need to train more."* Or, *"I was not able to be fast enough, it taught me that I don't have to be a perfectionist."* When you do that, you can visualize the image transforming into a magic stair. This object will be very useful in the future.

6. Go back to doing some "superhero's breaths". It's now time to become aware of the usefulness of transforming failures into magic stairs.

7. Imagine yourself in a big house where there is no staircase. Your goals, dreams and wishes that you cherish lie in a bedroom on the second floor. Always remember that a superhero finds all objectives noble and delightful. So your bedroom is really full of things, even tiny goals! It is very difficult to go there because this funny house doesn't have any staircase. Of course, nothing is ever really impossible - you can go looking for a hidden ladder or even attempt to jump, but it seems very tiring. With some stairs, life would be way easier.

But wait. Weren't you transforming your past failures into such objects a few minutes ago? Spend a few seconds processing your failures and observe a staircase appearing in front of you. As you transform more and more past failures with the magic formula, you are creating a complete staircase towards the building. Superheroes spend a lot of time doing this, but it proves to be worth it in the end.

If you do not have enough past failures in stock, you are allowed to use and imagine the failures of other people and transform them as well. The only rule is that you mustn't forget to apply the formula *"X has not been able to… X taught me that…"* Without this formula, it is impossible to create such objects with the sole power of one's mind, no matter how much power a superhero might have!

8. Note your breathing now. Take some time to take nice deep breaths in and out with your belly rising and falling. Note that as you're able to climb up the stairs, you are also able to see more

details in your dream. It's not unusual to realize that the actual aspect of the dream or goal wasn't quite what we first imagined. It's perfectly normal. Your bedroom is big enough to host many goals and dreams.

9. Visualize again a failure in the process of being transformed by the power of the *"I have not been able to… it taught me that…"* formula. This time the resulting stair appears with an unusual color. This is a sign that at the same time you were repeating this formula, I was helping you transform this past failure into a stair. Do not hesitate to ask your family members to help you transform your past failures into this powerful tool for achieving your goal. Funny enough, colored stairs are more solid and useful to see through goals and dreams. They are kind of « super-stairs ».

10. Now slow down the pace of your breathing gradually, become aware of your surroundings and gently open your eyes. You are making great steps in becoming invulnerable to failure. You are becoming as invincible as superheroes are. You may use this technique anytime.

- NAMASTE -

CHAPTER 6
UNBLOCK YOUR SUPER FORCE

Superheroes live intense lives; this is the least we can say. Whether they are fighting for justice or just training intensively, superheroes' forces are overstretched every day. Of course, their gifts give them great strength, but it is never enough. And even if they can purify their mind with the technique of "spontaneous sleep", it is still useful for superheroes to know techniques that can work in situations where sleeping is not an option.

Once again, the solution is to train the mind. Like you, the more superheroes train their mind, the stronger it will be able to help them to reach their goal. You are now going to learn a technique to regenerate yourself quickly by filling your body with a positive and powerful energy. Your body has energy reserves that you do not know of. Let's unblock them to make you ready for your next adventures.

1. As we learned before in the "superhero's breath" session, find a place where you can be seated or lie down feeling relaxed and comfy. Start to breathe at a normal pace, taking care of your belly swelling as you breathe in and deflating as you breathe out.

2. Now imagine a mountain setting in summer. The weather is hot and people are hiking and cycling; you notice many people having fun and enjoying this nice weather. Observe the beautiful nature around them. At the foot of this mountain, you know there is a secret location devoid of any human activity.

Go there. There is a clear stream and foliage with a fresh smell. Along the rocks of the mountain, there is a beautiful waterfall. Approach these rocks, but don't go under the waterfall yet. You can already feel the uniqueness of the warm water as you approach it. This amazing water is carried by a light breeze that refreshes your skin in the heat of the season.

3. Come closer to the waterfall until you are under it and let the torrent of water hit your body gently. Imagine your hands gently massaging your hair as it is washed by the pure water. Then feel this water sliding against your whole body and washing away the fatigue of the day.

4. Take a deep « superhero breath » while sliding this divine source on your belly, and it will wake up and regenerate your body and every muscle with it. Superheroes come here to find this positive energy after their most challenging fights. It gives them the strength to go forward. It is their necessary pair to the "spontaneous sleep" technique and other mind-training exercises.

5. Once your body feels refreshed by this cascade, lead yourself towards that flat rock along the river. Touch this unique rock with your hand. As soon as you touch it, you will feel that it is a rock like no other. This rock exudes a powerful energy and your hand is experiencing a delicious sensation of heat - the same kind of heat that you've just found under the waterfall and that you felt on your legs by going from the waterfall to this warming rock. It is said that this rock's energy is supplied by the visits of all the superheroes who come to visit it. Every time one comes, they leave some of their good intentions here. Every time one comes, the universe welcomes them by warming the scene with the intensity of a sun.

6. In this warm yet refreshing setting, now imagine your body lying on the rock where all superheroes come to relax by lying down.

7. Eyes closed, practice the « superhero's breath ». Feel how it is easier than usual to inflate your belly by inhaling the pure air of the waterfall and deflating with the exhaled air that has just passed through your purified and energized body. Practice this kind of breathing for a few seconds. It is so easy and it feels so good that you can even use your X-ray vision and scan your body while lying on the rock.

Calling the magic light of X-ray vision, feel the heat of the rock against your neck. Feel the heat of the rock against your back, against your backside, against your legs, against your calves. Let the positive heat radiate through your whole body and give it the superhero's power it needs. This energy is known as the « super-force ».

8. Now that your body is filled with this powerful energy, we are going to imagine that as you are laying a ball is located on your belly. Feel your breath making the ball move a little. Then take a small breath in, followed by a deep breath out so as to make your belly deflate to a wide extent. Then quickly inflate your belly with a rapid breath in to send the ball high in the sky. Your body has become as powerful as that!

9. Let's close this super-force meditation now by imagining yourself practicing your favorite sport with this superpower. Visualize how easy it is for you to achieve victory with the help of this new energy. Become aware that this mountain and this place is accessible any time. You just have to imagine the mountain and feel its power by closing your eyes for a moment and thinking about the waterfall and the fantastic warm rock.

10. After a few calmer breaths, you can open your eyes. You are ready for a fantastic adventure.

- NAMASTE -

CHAPTER 7
CALLING YOUR CONNECTION POWER

Today is the day for you to discover or practice a very nice superpower that superheroes must nurture with the greatest attention. The superpower I'm talking about is the *"connection power"*. The "connection power" is easy to understand: it simply means that we are all connected to each other by something very powerful. Whether things go well for superheroes or not, superheroes never forget this very powerful principle: that they live on this earth with other people who may differ in many ways from them, but who all share the fact of being alive with them.

Superheroes know how this life that is inside of them - just like in every other living being, plant or animal — feels, and how it vibrates in them. By taking the time to feel it on a deeper level, they stand ready to know when their life is being threatened.

Connected to the world and to the breath of life, superheroes can therefore intervene quickly to save this life force. Even when encountering situations where life disappears from one's body or when relatives do not survive their missions, superheroes know that nothing really goes away like that. By focusing on the breath of life, they know that it is powerful enough to bear all life.

The breath of life has been in all those people in the past; it crosses people today and it will cross people's bodies in the future. No matter what, the breath of life will remain the same, unique and very powerful, so it goes through everyone.

Today we are going to train your mind to feel this breath of life. We can't talk about a superhero training without knowing what you fight for!

1. As we learned before in the « superhero's breath » session, find a place where you can be seated or lie down feeling relaxed and comfy. Start to breathe at a normal pace, taking care of your belly swelling as you breathe in and deflating as you breathe out.

2. After taking care of the pacing of their breath, superheroes imagine their family and friends before them, smiling and breathing the same way they do. Do the same now. With closed eyes, imagine your loved ones and friends meditating like you, smiling and practicing the "superhero breath" with you. Together, your breaths are so strong that you will understand that the sound of their breaths is the sound of life itself. Thank this life for being in you and your loved ones, thank this life for allowing you to love and be loved; to have fun and to grow.

3. Now, imagine that with some superpowers you have discovered and thanks to the technical training of the mind you are able to teleport yourself and your loved ones onto a deserted island. On that island, there are no other things aside from luxurious vegetation and many wonderful animals. Teleported onto the sandy beach of this island, your faces get illuminated and warmed by the sun; you can even hear birds singing.

4. While you are sitting comfortably on the warm sand, imagine yourself waking up and looking to the sky. The bird that was singing is talking to you now. It asks you to follow it.

5. Take a few breaths to give yourself the courage and strength to follow the bird. As you follow the bird, you walk into the center of the island where the vegetation is the largest. The freshness of

the bushes caresses and refreshes your skin. The bird is not there, but you find a place where you can sit. This place is illuminated by some kind of light source from the sky. It is a fantastic skylight. Sit down there quietly.

6. You've just found the place where superheroes come to feel and honor life itself. It is said that this place is so full of great energy that it could be the energy center of the world. Everything that breathes and grows takes its source from the heart of the island where you are now sitting. Everything that has breathed in the past has witnessed the breath of life coming back to this place.

7. With your legs crossed, back straight, and sitting in a comfortable position, imagine yourself closing your eyes now as you are sitting in this illuminated place. Feel the breath of life in all the vegetation around you. Feel the energy of the trees around you, feel the life that spawns all the flowers and water lilies around you. Feel the life inside a small river near you. You cannot see the river, but you can hear it coursing; you feel the life inside it. The energy that you have felt before comes from there.

By focusing on this river that is unreachable by everything except for the force of the mind, superheroes strengthen their ability to feel the life connected to that river, and to feel the moment when this life force is threatened and wants to come back to the river.

8. Like superheroes, you are developing a superpower which enables you to feel this life energy, even in the most difficult periods of time. You shall return to this island to thank and honor life at any time you wish. Do not forget that even when everything seems lost, when everything seems to have disappeared, even when life has been taken away from a living being… life never actually disappears, but always returns to the river in the heart of this protected island, allowing the dense vegetation to grow, to renew itself and to give energy to the rest of the world.

9. Finish this meditation by thanking the connection aloud. Tell life, *"Thank you, life, for being in me and connecting me to others."*

CHAPTER 8
UNCOVERING YOUR POWER
OF AFFECTION

With the connection power meditation, we saw that superheroes have to train themselves to feel life everywhere so they are able to protect it better. But even if they can feel when life is about to leave someone and return to the island, or even if they have the strongest superpowers, it will do nothing if superheroes simply do not feel the need to save all mankind. To better feel this need and to serve the world, superheroes must train to feel affection for all beings. This affection may also be called « love ».

What makes superheroes help others - and what makes them do it well - is the feeling of love. Superheroes feel this love even when confronted by great moments of loneliness or when they feel that there are certain people who don't deserve their love.

Superheroes know that if they devote some time to take a few breaths and put their hands above their own hearts, they are able to feel all the people who possess such hearts. Let's practice this power of affection that no superhero can live without.

1. As we learned before in the "superhero's breath" session, find a place where you can be seated or lie down feeling relaxed and

comfy. Start to breathe at a normal pace, taking care of your belly swelling as you breathe in and deflating as you breathe out.

2. As superheroes do, gently put the hand of your choice above your heart. Take deep breaths, so that your connection with your heart will feel more vibrant and deeper. Remember that when you focus on one part of your body, your illuminating X-ray vision allows you to experience every beautiful corner of this part of you.

3. Imagine now that inside this heart live all the people who allowed you to exist, who feed you, who teach you new things, who help you grow and have fun every day. Superheroes often think of their friends, their allies, and their parents. Do the same for the people you love.

4. Feel their kindness and the energy they give you so that you feel good, safe and loved. Imagine their smiles, their hugs, the attention they give you to make you a healthy and happy human being. With your eyes closed and taking deep breaths, you can now feel your smile rising. Superheroes use all this generated love to gain courage and be successful.

5. Now let's dive deeper in the power of love. Are you ready? With your hand on your heart, think now of the people who don't love you that much in your opinion; think about people you have met and who have been mean to you. Remember that you are secure right now; we have just trained your mind to be as powerful as the minds of superheroes.

Now, be aware that these people are surely not in your heart right now - they might even have wounded your heart, so there is no reason to find them there. Do not worry, as we will not let them into your heart for the moment; your heart has no reason to welcome people who have hurt you or are likely to do so. Your heart is a sacred place where you can return to feel all the love that you deserve and that people give you. Yet we are to do something for these people who don't love you. Nothing mean, quite the opposite.

6. What we will do is very powerful, yet very simple. Just imagine that you put the hand you've just charged with love on the heart of the person with whom you feel no sense of love. Remember that these people are simply in need of love. By laying your hand on their heart, you give them some of your loving energy. You want them to feel what love can be like. As they'll become aware of the warmth of their heart, they eventually will not want to hurt any another heart - because every heart is sacred and they do not deserve to be damaged.

Superheroes have to practice such techniques in cases where the forces of evil would triumph and where it would be impossible to find the strength to move forward alone. Superheroes must train their mind to realize that all people have an unfailing love tank in them just waiting to be reactivated.

7. Imagine now that you rest your hand on your heart that contains the love of people you cherish. Take a few deep breaths to better feel this heart and love. You now know that you will never be alone because your heart is connected to everyone with the "power of affection". You can feel their presence at any time.

8. Now you also know that bad people are just lacking love, and you must hope that they also discover the magic of their heart one day.

- NAMASTE -

CHAPTER 9
SEEING THROUGH THE NIGHT

Superheroes are certainly endowed with superpowers and gifts that make them very special, but this does not always prevent them from feeling the bad emotions that we all feel. They also feel fear sometimes, especially early on in their careers when they are facing major obstacles for the first time. In such situations, they must take the time to develop a strong mind that helps them tame the fear and overcome it with great merits. To achieve this, superheroes must train their minds to create a light so strong that it brings down the fear.

Are you ready to create such light to be able to see clearly even when everything seems dark and threatening? Let's discover how you can do it!

1. As we learned before in the "superhero's breath" session, find a place where you can be seated or lie down feeling relaxed and comfy. Start to breathe at a normal pace, taking care of your belly swelling as you breathe in and deflating as you breathe out.

2. Once grounded with deep breathing, superheroes can use their mind to activate their magic light by repeating the following

formulas: *"Fears exist, nobody can tell me that my fear does not exist"*. Say it like a superhero *"Fears exist, nobody can tell me that my fear does not exist."* Take a deep breath and repeat after me now: *"Fears exist but I have a light in me stronger than all the fears. This light comes from my heart. My heart grows every day with all the love I give and receive. I know this light is stronger than all fears."*

3. Now imagine a castle in the dark night. See the tower that is lit by a large fire torch. You are standing at this tower, equipped with binoculars to see into the distance. You can feel a threat in the dark but you're safe on the tower of this castle, protected by strong fortifications and a powerful army. Your mission is to first assess the threat with your binoculars. Breathe deeply and look through the binoculars. Focus on what you see and try to assess the threat on a scale of 1 to 10. You're required to give the castle guards this vital information.

4. Know that it is in the very nature of fears that they become paralyzed when seen clearly. Fears benefit from shadows; they literally feed themselves from shadows. If you put enough light on fears, they can do nothing to you.

5. Once you have given the guards the information they need, it is time to put down your binoculars and breathe deeply so as to bring the light up in you. Repeat the formula: *"Fears exist but I have a light in me stronger than all the fears. This light comes from my heart. My heart grows every day with all the love I give and receive. I know this light is stronger than all fear."*

Feel the force of that light powering up all your body; feel it going out of you through your fingers. Direct your hand towards the threat and see the light radiating towards it. Do not forget that you gave the guards useful information on the threat. Remember that at your signal they are ready to help you. The guards can call their lights to help you trap the threat.

6. Imagine now that the guards are hearing your signal. They are now helping you with their own inner light. It is now a multitude

of lights that is heading to the threat to trap it. Soon, the threat will be useless without the darkness it needs to move forward. Congratulate yourself for having blocked the threat.

7. Young superheroes practice this exercise of night vision every time a new threat makes them tremble. They like taking the time to ground themselves, closing their eyes and imagining the castle and the tower. They like feeling the help of the binoculars and the guards. After their victory over the threat, superheroes take deep breaths and open their eyes slowly.

8. Before opening your eyes, you too should take a few deep belly breaths. It is from this area of your body that the source of all superpowers springs. Superheroes never abide by the law of fears, nor do they accept feeling worse just to avoid fear. Superheroes know that with the light of their allies and their own, they are going to be stronger than the fear. By preferring to call their light and not fight fear in the darkness, superheroes prove that they are truly special people. You are the same: every time you fight your fears with such practices, you are proving your exceptional nature to everyone.

9. Open your eyes now, feeling protected and safe.

- NAMASTE -

CHAPTER 10
THE MAGNETIC PROTECTIVE FIELD

The career of superheroes is not an easy path. It goes without saying that they can end up facing situations of extreme emergency where everything seems to collapse around them. In these times superheroes are required to respond immediately without taking the time to check that their bodies and minds are sufficiently aligned. Only an aligned body and mind can find an appropriate response to such situations.

Instead of reacting with anger, hatred and unnecessary violence towards themselves and others, superheroes know that they have to take the time to protect themselves and wait for things to calm down. They know not to rush. Superheroes are not brash; they are strategists. To master this effective protecting ability, a training technique is particularly suited for the mind. I call it the "magnetic protective field" meditation. You too are going to experience this wonderful protecting tool. You'll be able to use it as soon as you feel out of control and need some clarity.

1. As we learned before in the "superhero's breathe" session, find a place where you can be seated or lie down feeling relaxed and

comfy. Start to breathe at a normal pace, taking care of your belly swelling as you breathe in and deflating as you breathe out.

2. This time, rather than turning our attention to another part of the body, we are going to stay focused on your belly. The idea is to take such a grounded breath that it will create a protective magnetic field around you. While you are breathing, you will be safe. Trust me, every big superhero knows this technique.

3. Continue to breathe with the help of the "superhero's breath" technique. Take huge breaths by inflating the belly, and alternate with several deeper and slower exhalations by deflating the belly. Be sure to completely empty your stomach as you breathe out. That's it. Carry on that gentle yet powerful breathing.

4. Feel the source of all power that lies in your belly; feel the activation of your magnetic shield. Although tiny at first, your shield grows to create a very large field. You can even protect the people you want by placing them into the shield as you take larger, deeper breaths. Superheroes train this way in order to effectively protect their loved ones. Do the same if you wish. Take deep belly breaths to include all your loved ones.

5. Feel the security that you bring to yourself and your loved ones. Imagine a large gust of wind carrying objects with it that rise in the air. These objects are coming towards you dangerously. Still, imagine these objects bumping against the magnetic field that you've just created, strengthened with each breath you take.

6. With your eyes closed, breathe normally now. Your magnetic field is now sufficiently powerful to let you feel safe without having to make any effort. Feel the breath of fresh air that enables you to breathe, and gently touch your face. The magnetic field is not a prison; you can still interact with the world around you and feel its presence. Only items of pure negative energy will eventually bump on the magnetic shield.

7. Now you can feel the touch of fresh air that tickles your cheeks, gently raised by your smile. Rest and sit inside your magnetic field

until you feel completely safe. Rest there until you feel ready to peacefully govern what happens to you without anger, without hatred, without violent feelings towards yourself and towards others.

Superheroes do not like violence and they use it reluctantly. You should not think of wanting to use violence to imitate the superheroes. The truth is, superheroes really don't like violence - they just feel obliged to fight in certain situations to combat certain kinds of people that you don't meet in your life. Know that we cannot distinguish a hero and a villain from their use of violence, but we can do it by knowing that it's only heroes who genuinely love people and life.

8. With your calm mind, gently open your eyes and enjoy your state of being. You're safe. Your magnetic field is there with you all the time. When you feel that you are not connected to it anymore, do not hesitate to practice the magnetic shield meditation.

- NAMASTE -

CHAPTER 11
SUPER VISION

It is not uncommon that after all their battles, superheroes feel a void around them. Of course, their family and friends are never far away to celebrate the victory. But superheroes' adventures are often so extraordinary that they may have trouble finding interest in ordinary life events. Sometimes, they don't even know what to do with their time between missions. Then they feel a deep sense of boredom.

Today we will discover a very practical technique used by superheroes to fight against sadness during the empty days. This technique will allow you to develop powers you don't even suspect you have within yourself.

1. As we learned before in the "superhero's breathe" session, find a place where you can be seated or lie down feeling relaxed and comfy. Start to breathe at a normal pace, taking care of your belly swelling as you breathe in and deflating as you breathe out.

2. With your eyes closed and your belly filled with positive energy, now imagine your bedroom and all the stuff that is in it. Visualize your windows, your door, notice your mind's eye browsing the walls

and the floor, and observe the bed tracks, your games, your toys, and your clothes. Apply your super X-ray vision, calling your magic light to see the world around you.

3. The process is very simple for superheroes, so we'll do it like they do. One by one, silently pose questions to all the objects you've just observed. "Hey bed, how did you get here? What are you doing? Why are you in this form?", "Hey chair, how did you get here? What are you doing? What are you made of? How many people sat on you before me? "

4. With your eyes closed, sitting or lying down comfortably, now imagine yourself coming back to the windows. Now make your mind wander outside. Come here to ask trees their size, name and age, and ask the animals what they eat. By asking questions about everything they see, superheroes soon realize that things are much more interesting than they would have thought initially. Fighting and experiencing all kinds of action is not the only thing worthy of interest for them after all; the careful observation you are practicing now is also a superpower!

5. Always taking care to breathe like a superhero does, image a huge garden in front of you. Imagine literally that you *plant* all the questions you can ask in the ground - yes, that's right: take the question about the tree and bury it in the ground. Take the question about the chair and do the same with it.

6. After having buried all the questions inside this fertile ground, notice the full bucket of water waiting ready for you. Use it for watering all the things that you have buried before. Then, come and sit down on a bench. There you go, calmly observing the huge garden which bears no limit. Observe now, with more attention, the location that you have just worked on to grow your questions.

7. Observe those areas that do not change; observe others that are already giving birth to beautiful flowers, plants and shrubs. Observe the beauty of it. Smell the sweet and fresh fragrance of this vegetation.

8. Notice that the flowers are dancing now. Isn't it crazy? Dancing flowers! To the sound of quiet music, the flowers are indeed beginning to dance. Normally superheroes choose to watch this show, but sometimes they prefer to pick some flowers and offer them to someone, or use them to make a necklace. Superheroes can watch trees growing and make plans to build huts in them, or use fruits to cook wonderful meals. What will you decide to do?

9. After you have finished having fun in the garden, you can turn your focus back to your breath for a few moments. Then feel your head and thank it for having worked well, feel your body that has come to the garden and planted all the questions. Then, when you feel ready, open your eyes slowly. Boredom is not an issue for you anymore; you've just found the favorite activity of superheroes when they feel aimless - having fun in a limitless, magical garden.

- NAMASTE -

CHAPTER 12
SUPER TONGUE

Today we are going to explore a mind-building exercise that is a bit particular. It is based on the fact that superheroes must sometimes go without food for days. When the future of the planet is at stake, some sacrifices must be made.

To prepare for this possibility, superheroes practice what I call the "mindful eating". This exercise allows them to anchor the maximum of what constitutes as a dish in their mind in order to remember and nurture that memory. It helps them bear with the waiting until they have access to actual food. The exercise itself is very nice for superheroes. They discover a funny way to enjoy a meal.

So let us also try to have this kind of fun. I will describe instructions that you must follow when the time comes for your next meal.

1. For this session, make an effort to sit on a chair at a real table. The mindful meal is quite ineffective when practiced standing, walking or sitting on a sofa. Although many superheroes have actually tried this out, they pointed out the lack of success of their

attempt. Remember, the source of all superpowers located in your belly is always better used when your body is completely geared towards practice. Besides, a table and a chair are specially made for the time when you eat, aren't they?

2. Sit down and take some "superhero's breaths". Start breathing at a normal pace, taking care of your belly swelling with the air you take through the nose and deflating when you breathe out.

3. Now make a conscious choice to stay free of distraction during the meal. Your attention must be centered on the process of feeding itself, and believe me, there is a lot you have to refrain from doing. There is no need to turn on the TV or distract yourself with videogames or magazines.

4. If other people are sharing this meal with you, ask them to make the effort not to talk. We all need to focus on our practice and we will have much time to talk later. Be silent during the entire time you're eating. Don't worry! Not talking does not mean not having fun!

5. Before putting food in your mouth, pay particular attention to it and its form. Ask yourself why it has this form. Ask yourself whether it could not be otherwise.

6. Take small portions of that food. To eat mindfully like a superhero, you need to take the time to chew the food carefully so that it releases all its taste. Experience and feel its taste in every bite. Become aware that with each breath that you take, each bite is different yet identical to the others. Feel the food going from your mouth to your throat and your stomach. Feel the food nurturing your body and making it stronger.

7. Now, have a nice, warm thought for all the people who have worked hard to prepare this meal - farmers, producers, people in the grocery shop, the people who have worked to buy these products. Ask yourself where the product originally comes from. Superheroes know they get most strength from products that come from the earth, gardens, trees and vegetation because those are loaded with

the energy of our planet. A powerful energy that allows us all to be alive and standing.

8. Eat the different dishes slowly and appreciate the difference of each food on your tongue. Is it acidic? Is it sweet? Is it hard? Is it soft? Drink water between every dish and feel its purifying power. This water also comes from the earth (since Earth is mainly made of water), so it has a very high-energy power. Feel its freshness on your teeth. Feel this freshness rushing into your stomach.

9. Do you enjoy the way you eat? Your super tongue can communicate with the food and connect with it, it's fantastic! Remember that you get the most out of something when you focus on it! It's as simple as that. The stronger your mind is, the better. That's why superheroes practice all these exercises.

10. Finish your meal quietly and congratulate yourself for your work.

- NAMASTE -

CHAPTER 13
CONNECT TO THE SUPER HEARING

We are now going to get to know our mind better by developing a power that can save superheroes in the most difficult situations quite easily. You are aware that you can talk and interact with your classmates and your loved ones. The power of words is indeed very important and it can create any kind of emotion in you: joy, fear, sadness, etc. It can prompt laughter in you, as well as tears of love. Talking is important for superheroes and they talk on all kinds of occasions.

But when they are unable to speak, for example when held by a villain or when they don't want to be detected, superheroes cannot accept the idea of being without resources. The fate of the world is in their hands. This is when the listening skill is revealed to be useful.

Did you know that when you are feeling a bad emotion, you can listen to yourself talking loudly about this emotion? This will have a strong healing power. Superheroes know this; sometimes they don't even hesitate to shout about the superpower they use to awaken their full power. When you listen to others, you can understand them better and act accordingly. Superheroes who listen know where to go and why. They know what to avoid and how to do that, and that's all because of the conscious practice of listening.

1. As we learned before with the « superhero's breath », find a place where you can be seated comfortably or lie in a straight position. Choose the position where you feel the most relaxed. Start breathing at a normal pace, taking care to apply the superhero's breath, your belly swelling with the air you take in with the nose and deflating like a giant air balloon when you exhale through your mouth.

2. Listen now to the sound of your breathing. Is it light? Is it deep? Are you the only one breathing in the room you are in? It might not be the case! Listen to the breathing of other people in the room.

3. Close your eyes and focus a little more on your breathing. Then go find out what is making the most noise. Is it you? Is it someone else in another room? Are there outside noises? Can you hear cars or animals? Who makes the least noise? Training the ear to notice what makes less noise is very useful for superheroes. In an explosion or any scene of noisy action, superheroes should be able to focus their attention on smaller noises that can change everything. The breathing of a captured person, the one of a comrade in danger, the sound of a ticking bomb, or a building that is starting to crumble…. Refusing to let yourself be controlled by what makes the most noise is a major help. It preserves your mind and makes you able to keep control over your environment just like superheroes do.

4. Refocus now on your body. With your eyes closed, feel your breathing again. Can you hear your heartbeat? Try to listen to your heart. You can put your hands on your chest above your heart to help you. Sometimes, it is very soothing to listen to one's heartbeat. It is a little sound that can be heard all day, but we usually do not take the time to listen to it because other noises hide it.

5. Imagine now that you're talking to a friend or a relative. Try to visualize the gestures that go with your words. Are your hands in your pockets? Are they in the air? Visualize a smile. What type of news would put a smile onto your friend's face? Remember that what you do will not always be communicated through words and sounds. A baby can frown and carry out a message with its facial expression alone, and that does not apply just for babies!

You can say things with a smile, with big gestures in the air or a laugh. You can train yourself to communicate without speaking, just as a superhero who is captured would. With your eyes closed, imagine another way to say « thank you » that does not involve words. See how easy it is and how you can feel the strongest emotions thanks to it.

6. All these wordless communication techniques are based on listening and attention. Superheroes can listen very carefully. They know how to listen with nodding and smiling at the speaker, encouraging them to continue. Smile if you want this meditation to continue. Repeat after me: *« I listen carefully. My focus is on what surrounds me and not on my thoughts. »* Congratulations, your mind is slowly but surely evolving to be like the mind of the most trained superheroes.

7. Focus on your breaths that go in and out now, and try to listen to the things around you as well as what is happening inside you; pay particular attention to your body. Feel what moment is the best to open your eyes.

8. When you finally open your eyes, feel the calm that surrounds you and that can be found everywhere, provided that you listen carefully. Of course, calm noisiness is the quietest sound of all. The ability to pay attention to it in a noisy situation is difficult, but superheroes can do it - and you can do it too with some practice!

- NAMASTE -

CHAPTER 14
FOSTER A TEAM SPIRIT

There are other elements that make the life of superheroes difficult besides physical exertion and training. For example, they have to travel far from their home and family without knowing who they will encounter along the way. During their journey, superheroes are indeed likely to meet a wide range of people who sometimes prove to be amazing companions. Still, it is never easy to reach out to others.

To be certain that they partner up with the best people, superheroes must develop powerful mental techniques to make friends and not be afraid to reach out to others. Without it, they risk missing many opportunities to make their missions more fun. Because life is more fun for everyone when there are more people to share its joy with, we are going to learn how a superhero operates.

1. As we learned before in the « superhero's breathing », find a place where you can be seated comfortably or lie in a straight position. Choose the position where you feel the best relaxed. Start breathing at a normal pace, taking care to apply the breathing of a hero: the belly swelling with the air you take in with the nose

and deflating like a giant air balloon when you exhale through the mouth.

2. With your eyes closed and your body on the ground, imagine your friends before you. By « friends » I mean someone you know and like and who also appreciates you. Imagine these people you call friends. Look at their faces. Feel how easy it is to smile at a friend who smiles back at you. Also, feel how hard it is to smile when a friend is sad. It's simply a connection taking place between you. With connection, superheroes know when they can have fun and when they have to help their friends. Take a moment to imagine yourself enjoying playing games you like with the friends you are visualizing. Isn't it a pleasant feeling for the heart?

3. Now that your heart is warmed by friendship, try to think back to your first encounter with such a friend. Was it at a social event? Were you alone? Were you the one who made the first step? Is it the opposite? Now relive the magic of this first day. Maybe it was a long time ago when you were very young; perhaps you've forgotten. No need to worry. Just make sure that the next time this kind of first day comes, you really appreciate it so you can remember it easily later.

4. Now that your eyes are closed and your breathing is well anchored to the ground, imagine before you all the people you can see all day but whom you never go close to. Imagine all the people who have not approached you, whom you did not greet or who have not welcomed you.

While you're safe by practicing this exercise of the mind, imagine now going towards these people, not risking anything. Imagine talking to them about something, anything - perhaps a hobby of yours or a piece of information that you're interested in. Maybe you can tell a joke, ask a question or simply offer to play with them. Perhaps you could give the person a compliment on what they do or about how they are dressed.

Superheroes know to observe the qualities of each person whom they come across on the road. They do not hesitate to tell people about it politely and kindly. They know the power of an honest compliment; it helps generate and nurture a good friendship, like one would offer to share a sweet candy.

5. Come back now to your breathing for a moment and imagine the reaction of the person facing you as you're approaching them. Imagine a good reaction that leads you to other discussions or to other games. Take a deep breath in and breathe out. Now imagine yourself going on an adventure with that person. You can think of a movie you saw recently and imagine both of you as the heroes of this movie. Is it not fun? To get there, you first had to approach this person and show your interest in them, but wasn't it worth it?

6. Knowing they must find allies on their way, superheroes sometimes try to show off in order to impress people and feel well-liked. These superheroes then often end up greatly disappointed because those people who only show interest in someone because they are impressed by them don't come for who the person really *is*, but for what they *do*. In times of need, these people won't prove to be great, kind and helpful because they didn't come to keep company to the superhero who is imperfect and needs help - they want to be with them only when things are impressive and great.

7. After such a warning, keep in mind that superheroes normally end this meditation by thanking the universe for allowing them to come across so many people. They also thank loneliness for allowing them to find the time and quietness to train their minds, and for allowing them to be liked for this personal feature.

Do the same! Say thank you to loneliness, which is not an enemy of friendship, but it can help you grow by giving you the opportunity to enrich your personality and have plenty to share with the people on your path.

- NAMASTE -

CHAPTER 15
CONTROL TIME

Superheroes are often in places where there is little to do. Being captured by villains and thus waiting for their allies to come and save them is not rare. Superheroes may have to wait, sometimes for long periods of time. It is normal to feel impatient! Superheroes can feel the tension rising in their bodies, a little nervousness, a desire to stomp or scream at the universe. But they know that this way of handling things may have a bad influence on them. They know that sometimes we all need to accept that everything doesn't always depend on us. They know that the world is made up of different human beings who rely on each other to achieve things. Superheroes also know that those things that depend mainly on them sometimes require great efforts. After all, not many great things can be created in one day. True superheroes know that waiting is actually full of opportunities for them to reconnect with their minds and their bodies. So let's learn how to wait like a superhero.

1. As we learned before with the « superhero's breath », find a place where you can be seated comfortably or lie in a straight position. Choose the position where you feel the most relaxed. Start breathing at a normal pace, taking care to apply the superhero's

breath, belly swelling with air you take in through the nose and deflating like a giant air balloon when you exhale through the mouth.

2. With your eyes closed, imagine yourself in a standby situation, as many people are also waiting at the same time as you. Watch people turning around and starting to panic. Some of them are so mad they decide to leave, as if they had realized that their goals were not that important after all. Try to find out which way you usually wait for something or someone. Are you liking the boy who stirs? Or do you remain silent as the girl who sings quietly and smiles? Do you feel agitated? Try to find someone who reacts exactly as you would.

3. Now that your mind is receptive to the rising of its strength, discover what to do in this kind of situation where you need to wait. At first, it is useful to practice a few « superhero's breaths » again, but there is no need to sit or lie down this time.

4. Continue the deep breaths and start listening to your body. While waiting, your body will be your main focus; your mission will be to anchor it to the ground as much as possible by breathing through the belly. By doing so, you will be in a better condition for doing what you have come here to do. I call it « *listening to the radio of the body* », and you don't need headphones for it! Pay attention solely to your breathing.

5. What does the radio of your body say? Is your breathing quiet today? How do your hands feel? How do your back and feet feel? What emotions are the strongest in you? Feel the sense of expectation which becomes less and less unpleasant as you listen to your body and accept it as it is.

6. Continue to breathe in and out and connect yourself to the outside world by simply listening. Listening is one of the strongest of powers! We saw this in a previous lesson. What sounds can you hear? Have fun guessing their origin. If there are no noises at all, listen to silence. Feel its purity and the calm it brings to you.

7. Close your eyes and try to guess the activities of people in the room. Do they carry on doing what they were doing when you watched them the first time? Surely some of them have left; surely others are still waiting. There are few who have probably found what they came here for.

8. Now let's have a thought for great pyramids and large buildings or castles. Imagine tall trees before you and a big mountain; think of great works of art you may know. Think about all the things that haven't been made yet. Think of this book for example; think of the training heroes go through. Ask yourself: how much time did these things need to be created?

Superheroes ask themselves this question. This way they may realize that ultimately it is not a good question to ask. After all, the most important thing is to know that these things indeed exist, and that we all have to recognize their greatness. Knowing the age of a tree is interesting for some people. Feeling the freshness of its shadow is way more important for a greater number of people. With patience, the most beautiful things can emerge from the creating force of life.

9. With your eyes still closed, imagine the room again. Imagine that you are finally called. Relish having had to take this waiting time to reconnect to your body and to your mind.

- NAMASTE -

CHAPTER 16
BALANCED FEET

Superheroes are confronted by multiple tasks each day, and not all are easy to follow. Their superhero job takes a lot of time from their lives.

But superheroes might not want to devote their entire lives to saving the world. Sometimes they may want to be like everybody else and have fun with their friends or play sports. They might also want to study or work.

Superheroes sometimes feel torn between these different activities. They are sometimes tired of studying, and some other times they are tired of sports and events. On other occasions, they want to give up everything to dedicate themselves to the fight against evil. Occasionally these great people feel like they have to give up their superhero career and go back to being normal.

Yet superheroes know in their hearts that every individual task feels good after having taken the time to choose an activity they like, and which is compatible with their path in life. What might be missing is the ability to go from individual satisfactions to an overall sense of happiness and achievement.

To feel happiness over completing every likable activity, superheroes are well advised to use a practical training of the mind that is quite enjoyable. Let's practice it!

1. As we learned before in the « superhero's breath », find a place where you can be seated comfortably or lie in a straight position. Choose the position where you feel the most relaxed. Start breathing at a normal pace, taking care to apply the "superhero's breath", the belly swelling with the air you take in with the nose and deflating like a giant air balloon when you exhale through the mouth.

2. With your eyes closed and breathing smoothly, let's prepare for greeting the seven animals that superheroes derive their strength from. Whatever animal we are going to observe, remember that you're safe. We are going to approach these animals solely by the use of our mind. So let's relax and start with the salutation of the fox.

3. Imagine a fox on a mountain. Wave to the fox and observe it as it watches you while crossing a tiny river with many rocks. The fox is a symbol of an attentive mind. Superheroes welcome the fox for the strength it gives to their minds, helping them to be precise, sharp and focused.

4. Observe the fox as it hides in the forest now. A deer approaches you; it represents the heart. It reminds superheroes that careful work is not enough to create the necessary joy for their life. As we have already seen, superheroes - just like you - need to give and receive love, and connect with others.

Welcome the deer because it gives you the strength to show love and to receive it. It helps you connect with others and have fun. Now go deeper in the forest. Soon, you'll discover a giant pool of water.

5. There is a dolphin in this pool! Hear the cries of the dolphin as it greets you with its fin. Do the same and greet the dolphin. The dolphin is the symbol of health. By observing the dolphin, you

are training your mind to always pay attention to your body and emotions.

We carefully have to listen to our bodies and emotions. If you don't, they make themselves bigger and can be painful. Salute and thank the dolphin for helping you be in good health and for enabling people to be healthy. Greet the dolphin one last time, taking a deep breath to show it how the health and life that is within you resonate with it.

6. While you were greeting the dolphin, a lion approached you. Remember that you're safe. The lion is the symbol of work. Welcome the lion, as superheroes would. Superheroes know that a sharp mind is not everything, and that apart from love and attention to one's health, work is also needed to accomplish great things.

Without work and effort, superheroes would be weak and unfulfilled; they wouldn't achieve their ultimate state of being. This is not to say that work cannot be fun!

7. There is now an elephant approaching the lion. The elephant is the symbol of social connection. Welcome the elephant because it tells superheroes that the feeling of loneliness is never permanent and that we are all connected to each other.

8. Now greet the penguin, which has come to play with the elephant. It happens that penguins are the symbol of the family. Imagine your family before you and thank every one of them for bringing you solace, comfort and love.

9. Finally, celebrate the monkey that is also coming to play with the elephant. Without monkeys, things would be very sad. Even in the worst situations superheroes know how to find joy. Playful and fun moments are very important to superheroes; it regenerates their mind, keeping it fresh and illuminated. Cherish the time you spend with playing, because it's a very powerful time that allows you to restore your mental well-being.

10. Before concluding this meditation, imagine all the animals going back to the river with you where you had first seen the fox. All of them are greeting you, so welcome them back. Thank them for being in your life and make a promise that you will always protect them.

11. You can now open your eyes gently; your mind is on the right track to feel happiness when navigating through all your activities.

- NAMASTE -

ONE LAST THING...

If you enjoyed this book or found it useful, I'd be very grateful if you would post a short review on Amazon. Your support really does make a difference and I read all the reviews personally so I can get your feedback and make this book even better.

Thanks again for your support!

Louis LEGRAND

47281159R00035

Made in the USA
Middletown, DE
20 August 2017